How BIG Was Goliath?

Answers to a child's first Bible questions

THAT'S BIG!

By Betsy Rosen Elliot • Illustrated by Don Page

Who wrote the Bible?

Who wrote the Bible?
The Bible was written by different people whom God inspired. Some of these writers were great leaders like Moses and David. David was a shepherd who became a king!

What does *Bible* mean?
The word *Bible* comes from the Greek word *biblia*, which means *books*. The Bible is actually a collection of 66 books!

What is a prophet?

A prophet is someone who speaks for God. Sometimes a prophet tells us about the future. Isaiah wrote about the coming Messiah, God's special person. Other times a prophet tells the truth about right now. Nathan told David about the secret bad things God knew David was doing.

Why do we call the Old Testament *old*?

The Bible is made up of the Old and New Testaments. The whole book is old but when we talk about the Old Testament, we mean the old agreement between God and his people. When Jesus came, he gave us a new agreement: the New Testament.

Is Jesus in the Old Testament?

No...and yes! The Old Testament books don't name Jesus directly. But some books, like Isaiah and the Psalms, do tell us a lot about him. They call him the *Messiah*, or God's special person.

How did God make people?

How did God make people?
God made the first man, Adam, out of dust and breathed life into him. While Adam was sleeping, God took out one of his ribs and made it into the first woman, Eve.

GIRAF

WART. HOG

Where did Adam and Eve live?
Adam and Eve lived in a beautiful place called the Garden of Eden. There was a river flowing through it. Nobody knows exactly where Eden was, but many think it was in Iraq. There were many animals living in the garden and God let Adam choose their names!

What did Adam and Eve do wrong?

Adam and Eve disobeyed God. God told them that they could eat from every tree in the Garden except one in the center of the garden. A serpent convinced Eve that God was just being mean. So Adam and Eve ate the forbidden fruit. Their special friendship with God was badly hurt.

Did Adam and Eve have many children?

Adam and Eve had three sons that we know a little about. Cain, the oldest, was a farmer. The next son, Abel, was a shepherd. Cain got angry because God liked Abel's offering instead of his, so he killed Abel. The third son was Seth and he lived to be 912 years old!

How big was Noah's ark?

How big was Noah's ark?
The ark was 450 feet long (longer than a football field), 75 feet wide (put five cars end to end) and 45 feet tall (like a very big house)!

Did other people go into the ark with Noah?
Noah's wife and his three sons, Shem, Ham, and Japheth went. His three sons each took their wives as well. That made eight people in the ark.

How many animals went into the ark?
Noah took two or more of every kind of bird and animal that you can imagine, plus a few more! Nobody knows the exact number of animals altogether, but it must have been a pretty noisy ark!

How long did it take Noah to build the ark?

It probably took Noah about 120 years to build the ark! And Noah was about 480 years old when God told him to start building! He was 950 years old when he died.

WHEW!!!

Why did God make a flood?

People were doing bad things. They cheated and hurt each other. They didn't worship God. And they didn't care for the earth. God was sad he had ever made people and he decided to start over.

ARE WE THERE YET?

When did the first rainbow appear?

God sent the first rainbow after the flood. It was a sign of his promise to Noah that he would never again flood the whole earth. So whenever you see a rainbow, you know that however much it rains, God has promised he won't let it rain so much that it will flood the whole earth!

What was so amazing about Joseph's coat?

What was so amazing about Joseph's coat?
Joseph's coat had many colors. Clothes in those days were not colorful like they are today so it would really have stood out! But the coat was special because his father, Jacob, gave it to him. It showed how much his father loved him.

Why were his brothers jealous?
Joseph was Jacob's favorite son and Jacob's other sons were jealous. They also hated Joseph's dreams about how he would one day be the boss. They were so upset they threw him in a pit and sold him as a slave to Egypt.

Why were dreams special to Joseph?
Joseph's dreams were messages from God about the future. In Egypt, God told him that Pharaoh's dreams about cows and grain were a warning about a famine, or shortage of food, to come.

What did Joseph do in Egypt?
Potiphar bought Joseph as a slave but soon put him in charge of his household. Potiphar's wife lied about Joseph and he was unfairly put in prison. But he was freed so he could explain Pharaoh's dream. Pharaoh was so impressed, he put Joseph in charge of everything in Egypt!

Did he ever see his brothers again?
There was a famine everywhere. But in Egypt, Joseph had stored plenty of food ahead of time. Egypt sold food to other countries. So Jacob sent his sons to Egypt to buy grain. Joseph told them who he was and the family came together again. Jacob, his sons and their families moved to Egypt.

Can a bush really talk?

Can a bush really talk?

Bushes can't talk unless God chooses to make them! He did with Moses. Moses saw a bush on fire, yet it didn't burn up! The bush started calling his name. It was really God who used the bush to get Moses' attention. God wanted Moses to know that his people would soon be free.

Why was baby Moses in the bulrushes?

God's people were slaves in Egypt, and Pharaoh ordered all their boy babies to be killed. He was afraid they would grow up to fight him. So Moses' mother hid him in a basket and floated it on the Nile River by the bulrushes, or reeds. When Pharaoh's daughter came to bathe at the river, she found Moses. Moses' name means *taken out of the water*.

What was *manna*?

The first time God's people saw this stuff on the ground they asked, *manna*? In Hebrew this means, *What is it?* God's people wandered in the desert for 40 years before they reached the Promised Land. There weren't any grocery stores so each morning God gave them white, breadlike stuff. It tasted like wafers made with honey. The name stuck and they called it *manna*.

Why didn't God's people just swim across the Red Sea?

Swimming would have been hard for the Israelites in regular clothes and when they were carrying things! Instead, God helped them escape from the Egyptians by making a great wind push the water back to make a path to the other side. But when the Egyptians tried to cross, the water came back and drowned them. God chose to do a special miracle to save his people so that their faith would grow.

Special people and animals

Are there any famous children in the Bible?
Joash was only seven years old when he was crowned king! Esther has a whole book written about her. She was an orphan and a Hebrew slave who became a queen of Persia! Samuel was only a boy when God first called him to become a prophet.

HI, GUYS

?

!

!

Are there any famous animals in the Bible?
The lion is mentioned most in the Bible. Sheep also appear often. The eagle was considered special because of its strength and speed. When Elijah hid in the desert, ravens brought him food every day. One time, Balaam's donkey talked and tried to warn him about an angel in the road!

How did David, a shepherd, become a king?
When Saul stopped being a good king, God sent the prophet Samuel to David's family. David's seven brothers seemed more like kings than David, the youngest. But God told Samuel that the young shepherd really loved God. Then Samuel poured oil on his head, and David went to serve Saul. David became king after Saul died.

WOW!

How did Joshua win the battle of Jericho?

God told Joshua to trust him and to have all the people march around the city of Jericho once a day for six days. Then on the seventh day, they were to march around the city seven times while the priests blew trumpets. The people obeyed God, and then shouted loudly, and the walls of Jericho tumbled down!

Why was Daniel thrown to the lions?

Why was Daniel thrown to the lions?
Daniel was being punished because he wouldn't stop praying to God. Darius, King of Babylon, had been tricked into making a law against praying to anyone but him. Darius tried to keep Daniel from the lions, but he was forced to follow his own law when Daniel kept right on praying.

Why didn't the lions eat him?
Daniel came out without a scratch because God protected him. God sent an angel to shut the lions' mouths. King Darius was so amazed that he made a new law: everyone in his kingdom had to worship Daniel's God!

Why was Daniel in Babylon?

Daniel was captured and taken prisoner. He was probably a teenager when he was taken to Babylon. He was from one of the royal families of Judah and was handsome and smart. King Nebuchadnezzar trained Daniel for three years before Daniel could serve him. Daniel was about 70 when he was thrown to the lions.

What happened to Daniel's friends?

Shadrach, Meshach, and Abednego were thrown into a fiery furnace because they would not worship a gold statue of the king. They came out alive, without a single burn, because God protected them. God sent someone special to walk in the flames with them.

How big was the big fish?

How big was the big fish?
The big fish that God sent to swallow Jonah might have been a whale. It was large enough for Jonah to live inside for three days and nights!

Why was Jonah running away?
God had a job for Jonah. He was to go to Nineveh, the capital of the enemy nation, Assyria. God wanted Jonah to tell the people to follow God, but Jonah ran away. He didn't want to help his enemies.

What happened to Jonah?
Jonah got on a ship. Then God made a terrible storm and the ship was about to sink. Jonah knew that the storm was his fault because he was running away from God. He begged to be thrown overboard. Immediately the storm stopped. Then God sent a big fish to save Jonah.

How come Jonah didn't suffocate inside the fish?

God wasn't finished with him yet. Jonah prayed from inside the fish, thanking God for saving him. God then told the fish to spit Jonah onto dry land.

Did people listen to Jonah after he got out of the fish?

Jonah went to Nineveh and told them, "Forty more days and Nineveh will be destroyed." The people listened and were sorry. When God saw how they changed, the city was spared.

Record breakers!

How strong was Samson?

Very strong! One day he defeated a lion with his bare hands. Soon after, he fought 30 men at one time and won! Another time, he defeated 1,000 men with a donkey's jawbone. Samson was so strong, he was able to push the pillars of a temple so that it came crashing down.

Who was the smartest person in the Bible?

King Solomon was the most famous for his wisdom. When he became king of Israel, God asked him what he would like for a gift. Instead of asking for riches, Solomon asked for an *understanding heart* and a mind to know right and wrong. God gave him what he wanted. We can see his wisdom in the book of Proverbs, for example.

HE'S SMART!

How big was Goliath?

The Philistine giant was over nine feet tall. His helmet and his armor were made of bronze. The huge spear that he carried had a 25-pound spearhead.

THAT'S BIG!

Who was the oldest person in the Bible?

Many people in the Bible lived to be much older than people do today. Methuselah, who was Noah's grandfather, was 969 years old when he died!

Who was the youngest king in the Bible?

Joash was seven years old when he became king. He was faithful to God, but he didn't make any real changes to help people follow God.